SPORTS' ONE-HIT
WONDERS

BY THOMAS CAROTHERS

SportsZone

An Imprint of Abdo Publishing
abdopublishing.com

abdopublishing.com

Published by Abdo Publishing, a division of ABDO, PO Box 398166, Minneapolis, Minnesota 55439.
Copyright © 2018 by Abdo Consulting Group, Inc. International copyrights reserved in all countries.
No part of this book may be reproduced in any form without written permission from the publisher.
SportsZone™ is a trademark and logo of Abdo Publishing.

Printed in the United States of America, North Mankato, Minnesota
102017
012018

THIS BOOK CONTAINS
RECYCLED MATERIALS

Cover Photos: Frank Franklin II/AP Images, foreground; Paul Sancya/AP Images, background
Interior Photos: Nick Wass/AP Images, 4; Roberto Borea/AP Images, 6–7; Terry Renna/AP Images, 9; Tony
Avelar/AP Images, 10; Mark J. Terrill/AP Images, 12; Chris Carlson/AP Images, 13; Takeo Tanuma/Sports
Illustrated/Getty Images, 14; Sadayuki Mikami/AP Images, 16, 17; AP Images, 18–19, 27, 28, 29; Bettmann/
Getty Images, 20; John Iacono/Sports Illustrated/Getty Images, 21; Rick Stewart/Getty Images Sport/
Getty Images, 23; Al Behrman/AP Images, 24; Rusty Kennedy/AP Images, 25; Bill Kostroun/AP Images, 30,
32; Frank Franklin II/AP Images, 33; John Gress/AP Images, 35; Eric Cable/AP Images, 36; Tim Wimborne/
Reuters/Newscom, 39; Matt Slocum/AP Images, 40; David Duprey/AP Images, 42; Ross D. Franklin/AP
Images, 43; Charlie Neibergall/AP Images, 44

Editor: Patrick Donnelly
Series Designer: Craig Hinton

Publisher's Cataloging-in-Publication Data

Names: Carothers, Thomas, author.
Title: Sports' one-hit wonders / by Thomas Carothers.
Description: Minneapolis, Minnesota : Abdo Publishing, 2018. | Series: The wild world of sports | Includes
    online resources and index.
Identifiers: LCCN 2017946937 | ISBN 9781532113697 (lib.bdg.) | ISBN 9781532152573 (ebook)
Subjects: LCSH: Sports--United States--History--Juvenile literature. | Sports--Miscellanea—Juvenile
    literature.
Classification: DDC 796--dc23
LC record available at https://lccn.loc.gov/2017946937

TABLE OF
CONTENTS

BRADY'S BUNCH
OF BLASTS

A long-held belief in baseball is that power is the last skill a hitter develops. In Brady Anderson's case, power didn't come for nine seasons.

Anderson played outfield for the Baltimore Orioles for most of the 1990s. With his trademark sideburns and hustle, Anderson was a favorite of Orioles fans throughout the decade.

But Anderson falls into a special class of athletes for whom, when you hear their name, you think of one amazing achievement. It could be a single game, a tournament, or even a season. But for that one moment in the sun, these athletes could do no wrong.

Anderson was more than a one-hit wonder. You might argue that he could be better known as a 50-hit wonder. That's because he hit a jaw-dropping 50 home runs in 1996.

Brady Anderson watches one of his 50 home runs in 1996.

Anderson was not much of a power hitter before that season. He had hit only 72 total homers in eight seasons up to that point. In 1995 he hit 16 home runs. In 1997 he hit 18. But that year in between was one to remember.

Just 29 games into the 1996 season, Anderson had already blasted 15 home runs. He had 30 at the All-Star break in early July. That helped him get voted into the starting lineup for the American League (AL) All-Star team.

Anderson didn't stay on the same pace in the second half of the season. But he didn't disappear, either. The Orioles rolled into Toronto for the season's final series with Anderson sitting at 47 home runs. He hit three homers against the Blue Jays in the last four games. He hit No. 50 in the first inning of the final game of the season. That gave him Baltimore's single-season record for home runs at the time.

Anderson's breakout season happened during what is now often referred to as the "Steroid Era" in Major League Baseball (MLB). Home run totals spiked in the late 1990s and early 2000s. Many players later admitted to using performance-enhancing drugs, but Anderson always denied the use of such substances.

As quickly as Anderson's power stroke arrived, however, it disappeared. When healthy, Anderson remained a productive player for Baltimore, but he never approached 50 homers again. He retired in 2002 with 210 career home runs, nearly a quarter of them coming in that one magical season.

ROOKIE RACER

Trevor Bayne was just one day past his 20th birthday when he shocked the world of auto racing. Making just his second NASCAR Cup Series start, Bayne became the youngest winner of the sport's biggest race. He won the Daytona 500 on February 20, 2011.

The race featured 74 lead changes and 22 different leaders. Bayne didn't find himself out in front of the pack until just two laps remained in the 208-lap race. He got there after the previous leader, David Ragan, was penalized. Ragan broke a rule and was forced to make a pit stop, putting Bayne in the lead. The rookie held the lead for the final two laps and took home the checkered flag.

Bayne broke Jeff Gordon's record as the youngest Daytona 500 champion by five years. Gordon went on to a standout racing career after winning his first Daytona 500 in 1997. But through 2016, Bayne had yet to win another race in the top flight of NASCAR.

Trevor Bayne was on top of the world after winning the 2011 Daytona 500.

CHEECHOO'S CHARGE

Hailing from Moose Factory, Ontario, Canada, Jonathan Cheechoo was a goal-scoring machine for the San Jose Sharks in the 2005–06 season.

The Sharks selected the 18-year-old in the second round of the 1998 National Hockey League (NHL) draft. He made his NHL debut in 2002. And he quickly became a fan favorite. Cheechoo scored a league-high 56 goals in 2005–06. His emergence helped energize the team and its fan base after the NHL lockout. That work stoppage had resulted in the cancellation of the 2004–05 season.

Cheechoo's 56 goals and 37 assists that season didn't appear to be a fluke. He scored 37 goals and added 32 assists the next year. However, Cheechoo got further and further from his 93-point peak as the seasons passed. He scored 23 goals in 2007–08 and just 12 the next year. By the 2009–10 season, the Sharks had traded him to the

Jonathan Cheechoo celebrates a goal in April 2006.

Cheechoo flips a backhander at an open net against the Los Angeles Kings.

Ottawa Senators. A year after that, he was out of the NHL for good after scoring just five goals in 61 games for the Senators.

Cheechoo bounced around the minor leagues for a few seasons before he moved overseas to play in Russia and in Europe, where he was still playing in 2017.

JUNEAU'S JOLTS

Joe Juneau joined the Boston Bruins immediately after playing for Canada's silver medal-winning team in the 1992 Winter Olympics. He was widely hyped as the Bruins' next great player. And he lived up to the hype by scoring 32 goals with 70 assists in his rookie season of 1992–93. But Juneau's scoring touch faded almost as quickly as it had emerged. He was traded to the Washington Capitals before the end of his second season in Boston. He scored just 62 total goals over the next six seasons. He became known as a strong defensive player but never regained his rookie scoring form. He finished a 14-year NHL career with 156 goals. Twenty percent of those came during his rookie season.

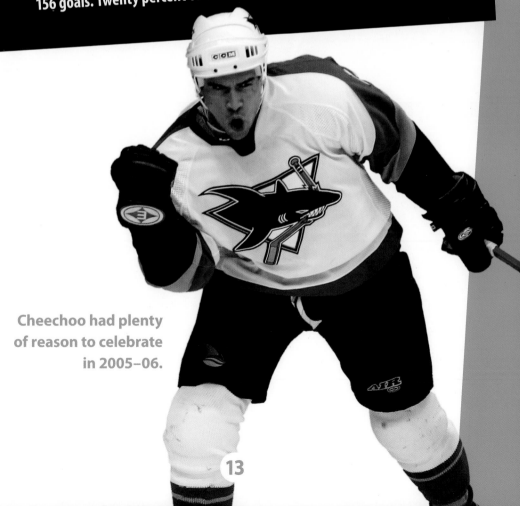

Cheechoo had plenty of reason to celebrate in 2005–06.

TOPPLING TYSON

Boxing is a sport known for stunning upsets. But nobody was prepared for what happened on February 11, 1990. That night, Buster Douglas shocked the world by beating Mike Tyson for the world heavyweight title.

Douglas entered the bout as a 42-to-1 underdog. He had a career record of 29–4–1 as he entered the ring at the Tokyo Dome in Japan. Tyson was at the height of his devastating powers. He was 37–0, and he had made a habit of ending bouts in less than a minute. Few thought Douglas stood a chance.

However, Douglas went toe to toe with the champion. As round after round went by, it became clear that Tyson wasn't going to cruise to an easy victory. He was locked in a struggle to save his title.

Douglas recovered from an eighth-round knockdown to send Tyson to the mat in the 10th round. It was the first time Tyson had

Buster Douglas lands the punch that sent Mike Tyson to the canvas in the 10th round of their heavyweight title match.

been knocked down in his professional career. He was unable to get up off the canvas before being counted out. Douglas stunningly became the new heavyweight champion.

Douglas, *right,* lands a punch to Tyson's face.

Douglas salutes the crowd as he leaves the ring as the new heavyweight champion of the world.

Douglas had a short reign as champion. He lost to Evander Holyfield in his first title defense on October 25, 1990. The fight lasted just three rounds before Holyfield knocked out Douglas to take over as the new champion.

Douglas left boxing after the fight. He attempted a comeback in 1996 but officially retired as a boxer in 1999.

THE BIRD
TAKES FLIGHT

Mark Fidrych baffled and enchanted the baseball world in the summer of 1976. As a rookie pitcher with the Detroit Tigers, Fidrych went 19–9. He led the AL with a 2.34 earned-run average (ERA) and 24 complete games. His tremendous stats were coupled with a gigantic personality. The combination quickly made him one of the most popular players in baseball.

Tigers fans delighted in his on-field antics, which included talking to the baseball in his hand and grooming the pitcher's mound by hand between innings. His enthusiasm was matched by his talent. Fidrych won the 1976 AL Rookie of the Year Award and was named to the AL All-Star team in each of his first two seasons.

One of the highlights of his rookie season was beating the mighty New York Yankees on June 28. The game was nationally televised

Mark Fidrych showed off his unique personality while pitching for the Detroit Tigers.

by ABC. Fidrych shut down the eventual AL champions for his seventh straight victory. He earned AL Player of the Month honors in June on the strength of a 6–0 record with a 1.99 ERA and five complete games.

He was nicknamed "The Bird" because he resembled Big Bird from TV's *Sesame Street*. Fidrych and Big Bird together graced the cover of *Sports Illustrated* in June 1977.

However, by that time, Fidrych's career was beginning to fall apart. At Detroit's spring training in 1977, he was catching fly balls during batting practice when he stepped wrong and tore cartilage in his left knee. Surgery sidelined him until late May. Two months later he injured his right shoulder and was never the same again. He threw 250 1/3 innings in 1976, but only 162 innings from 1977 until his major-league career ended in 1980.

Fidrych attempted to keep his career alive in the minor leagues over the next few years. But he never made it back to the big leagues, officially retiring in 1983.

Fidrych often dropped to his hands and knees to groom the pitcher's mound.

SHUFFLING STAR

Elbert L. Woods is better known as "Ickey" by fans of the National Football League (NFL). The dynamic running back burst onto the NFL scene in 1988 with the Cincinnati Bengals. After not seeing much action in his first three games, Woods scored his first two NFL touchdowns in a Week 4 game against the Cleveland Browns. That was just a sign of things to come.

Two weeks later, in a home game against the New York Jets, Woods made his permanent mark on the league. After scoring the first of his two touchdowns that day, Woods stood in the end zone. He hopped from one foot to the other while waving the ball. Then he spiked it. The dance quickly became known as the "Ickey Shuffle." It became a nationwide phenomenon.

NFL officials weren't big fans of the Shuffle, however. Some argued that Woods was violating league rules against taunting.

The "Ickey Shuffle" turned little-known running back Ickey Woods into a household name in 1988.

Woods, *center,* and his Bengals teammates show off their dance moves at Super Bowl Media Day on January 17, 1989.

So Woods shifted the celebration to the area behind Cincinnati's bench. That move satisfied the league.

Woods rushed for 1,066 yards and 15 touchdowns during the 1988 regular season and continued to perform the Shuffle to the delight of Bengals fans. He also rushed for 228 yards and three more touchdowns in the playoffs to help the Bengals reach the Super Bowl. But Cincinnati lost to the San Francisco 49ers, and Woods did not get a chance to perform the dance on the NFL championship stage.

Unfortunately, Woods's rookie season was also his best. Just two games into the 1989 season, he tore a ligament in his left knee. He was sidelined for more than a year. He played in 19 games over the 1990 and 1991 seasons but was unable to recapture his rookie form. The Ickey Shuffle was performed for the last time after a 1-yard touchdown run in a game at Miami on December 9, 1991.

Woods burst through a hole in the 49ers' defensive line during the Super Bowl.

PITCHER PERFECT

The history of baseball is filled with stories of unexpected heroes coming up big in historic moments. The most famous of all these was Don Larsen.

Not much about Larsen's career is noteworthy. He was a journeyman pitcher who played for seven teams between 1953 and 1967. His career win-loss record was 81–91. If not for the biggest day of his professional life, Larsen likely would have faded from memory. However, on that day, he pitched the only perfect game in World Series history.

The date was October 8, 1956. Larsen drew the start in Game 5 for the New York Yankees. They were facing their crosstown rivals, the Brooklyn Dodgers. It was Larsen's second start in the series. In Game 2, he didn't even make it through the second inning. He was sent to the showers after walking four batters and allowing four unearned runs.

But Game 5 was something very different indeed. Larsen baffled the Dodgers, not allowing a hit or walk while striking out seven batters over nine innings. The Yankees won 2–0, taking a 3–2 series lead on their way to winning the championship in seven games.

Don Larsen delivers a pitch during his perfect game in the 1956 World Series.

Larsen's place in history was suddenly assured. Through 2016 his performance remained the lone perfect game in World Series history. It was also the only no-hitter in postseason history until Roy Halladay of the Philadelphia Phillies no-hit the Cincinnati Reds in the 2010 playoffs.

The performance was the high-water mark of Larsen's career. He won 25 games over the next three seasons with the Yankees before he was traded to the Kansas City Athletics in 1959.

Larsen never won more than eight games in a season after that, as he bounced from team to team. His career came to an end after making three brief relief appearances for the Chicago Cubs in the summer of 1967.

Yankees catcher Yogi Berra (8) leaps into Larsen's arms after the game's final out.

LINSANITY REIGNS

When Jeremy Lin graduated from Harvard University, no pro basketball teams seemed to want him. He spent a couple of seasons bouncing around the National Basketball Association (NBA) and its developmental league. He also played in China.

He started the 2011–12 season with the Golden State Warriors. But in December, he was on the move again. The New York Knicks needed another point guard. Finally, Lin was in the right place. It soon became clear he was there at the right time, too.

Lin did not see much playing time in New York until February and was nearly released by the team. However, with Knicks head coach Mike D'Antoni desperate to break his team out of a long losing streak, he began to play Lin.

Lin responded by averaging 26.8 points as the Knicks won five in a row after losing 11 of their previous 13 games. He became an

Jeremy Lin turned around the New York Knicks' fortunes in 2012.

31

Lin quickly became a favorite of fans in New York and around the league.

overnight sensation, and his jersey quickly became the No. 1 seller among NBA fans.

Sportswriters began calling the hype around the young Knicks star "Linsanity." His play captivated New York and the NBA as a whole. Lin helped lead the Knicks to a 36–30 record and a spot in the 2012 playoffs.

The Miami Heat defeated the Knicks in the first round. With Linsanity still in the air, Lin made the most of his celebrity by signing a free-agent contract with the Houston Rockets.

Although Lin started all 82 games for the Rockets in the 2012–13 season, he was not the player he was with the Knicks. His scoring and assist totals slipped over two seasons in Houston. He bounced around the league, playing with four teams over five years as he returned to his pre-Linsanity journeyman status.

Lin fights through the defense of Lakers guard Derek Fisher.

LONG-SHOT LUNKE

Hilary Lunke had been on the Ladies Professional Golf Association (LPGA) Tour for a year when she entered the 2003 US Women's Open. She had not yet finished in the top 10 of an LPGA event. Approximately a month earlier, she had finished in a tie for 37th place in the LPGA Championship.

But for four days in July 2003, Lunke placed herself among the best. In what became her only LPGA title, as well as her only top-10 tour finish, Lunke won the US Women's Open title in a playoff against Angela Stanford and Kelly Robbins.

Lunke was tied for ninth place at even par after the first round, but she climbed into second place at the end of the second round at 2 under par. After the third round, she was in first place at 5 under.

Trouble hit on Sunday. Lunke shot a 4-over 75 in the final round. That pulled her back into a tie with Stanford and Robbins at 1 under

Hilary Lunke follows through on a shot during the third round of the 2003 US Women's Open.

for the tournament. The trio held off two-time Open champion Annika Sörenstam, who finished one shot back.

In the 18-hole playoff round Lunke seized what would become her lone tour victory by shooting a 1-under 70. Through 16 holes she and Stanford were tied at even par, three shots ahead of Robbins. Then Stanford bogeyed No. 17, giving Lunke a one-shot lead. Lunke clinched the win with a birdie putt on the final hole.

Family life called Lunke in the years after her Open win. She gave birth to her first child in 2007 and retired from professional golf in 2008 with one very big triumph to highlight her career.

BIRDIE'S BREAKTHROUGH

Two years after Lunke won the US Women's Open, the tournament crowned another one-year wonder as champion when Birdie Kim won the event. Kim had just changed her first name from Ju-Yun to Birdie the previous year. Then, at the age of 23, she won the Open with a 3-over score of 287. Kim's biggest shot was a 60-foot chip out of a bunker that dropped in the hole for her namesake—a birdie—helping her to her only LPGA Tour victory.

CHAPTER 10

OUTBACK UPSET

Chris O'Neil stunned the tennis world as the longest of long shots to win the championship of a Grand Slam tournament. The Australian won the 1978 Australian Open, becoming the first unseeded woman to do so.

Her feat remained unmatched until Serena Williams—a past champion returning to form after an injury—won the Australian Open as an unseeded player in 2007.

O'Neil came out of nowhere to storm through the field in 1978, despite being ranked just No. 111 in the world at the time. She did not lose a set in any of her seven matches. She clinched the championship with a 6–3, 7–6 win over American Betsy Nagelsen.

The Australian Open championship was the only singles title of O'Neil's career. She finished her career with a singles record of 19–52. She also posted a doubles record of 64–82, pairing with Pam Whytcross to win the 1983 Japan Open doubles title.

Chris O'Neil, *left*, poses with Serena Williams in 2007 after Williams became the first unseeded player to win the Australian Open since O'Neil had done it in 1978.

O'Neil retired in 1983. After her playing days were over, she began to coach tennis. She opened a tennis school near her hometown of Newcastle in New South Wales, Australia, where she can tell her students about her one great triumph.

TYREE'S TIME

David Tyree played five NFL seasons as a backup wide receiver and special-teams player with the New York Giants. Then one play in the Super Bowl made him a household name.

Tyree had long excelled for the Giants on special teams. He was even selected to play in the 2006 Pro Bowl because of his excellence in covering kickoffs and punts. He had never caught more than 19 passes in a season. In the 2007 season, which led up to Super Bowl XLII, he had caught only four passes with no touchdowns.

The Giants faced the undefeated New England Patriots in the Super Bowl. Tyree caught a 5-yard touchdown pass from quarterback Eli Manning to give the Giants a 10–7 lead early in the fourth quarter.

But the Patriots reclaimed the lead, setting the stage for the play of Tyree's career. With just over a minute left in the fourth quarter, he

David Tyree, *far left*, makes the catch that would come to define his career.

Eli Manning (10) gets ready to launch his long pass to Tyree.

leapt high and caught a 32-yard pass from Manning, pinning the ball between his right hand and his helmet.

That play, known simply as the "Helmet Catch," put the Giants deep in Patriots territory. New York scored the winning touchdown four plays later, ending New England's hopes of an undefeated season.

SUPER SURPRISE

Timmy Smith was a little-used rookie running back for the Washington Redskins, but on January 31, 1988, he made the biggest of splashes on the biggest of stages. Smith found out just minutes before the Super Bowl that he would be making his first NFL start. He went on to set a Super Bowl record with 204 rushing yards. He also scored two touchdowns as Washington stomped the Denver Broncos 42–10. Smith played in just 15 more games after the Super Bowl, gaining a total of 161 yards before retiring in 1990.

The Helmet Catch marked the high point of Tyree's career. A knee injury kept him sidelined for the 2008 season. He played one season with the Baltimore Ravens in 2009 before retiring.

Manning and Tyree celebrate after the Giants' shocking upset of the Patriots.

CHAPTER 12

TIGER TAKEDOWN

Even many golf fans didn't know much about Y. E. Yang when he arrived in Minnesota for the 2009 PGA Championship. At the age of 37, the South Korean golfer had spent the majority of his career playing in events outside the United States.

Yang had never finished higher than 30th in a major tournament before the 2009 PGA Championship. However, after four days of play at Hazeltine National Golf Club, Yang lifted the trophy as champion.

Ranked No. 110 in the world at the time, Yang became the first Asian-born player to win a major. What's more, he defeated the legendary Tiger Woods to do so. Woods was the No. 1-ranked golfer in the world and at the peak of his powers at the time. He also had won four PGA Championship titles before Yang defeated him.

The victory did not translate to further PGA Tour success for Yang. His best result in a major after 2009 was a tie for third in the 2011 US Open. Yang never won another PGA Tour event.

Y. E. Yang celebrates his victory over Tiger Woods and the rest of the field at the 2009 PGA Championship.

GLOSSARY

birdie
A score 1 under par on a golf hole.

checkered flag
A flag of black and white squares that is waved when the winner of an auto race crosses the finish line.

complete game
A baseball game in which the starting pitcher finishes the game.

earned-run average
A statistic that measures the average number of earned runs that a pitcher gives up per nine innings.

Grand Slam
Refers to the four major tennis tournaments in a year: the Australian Open, the French Open, Wimbledon, and the US Open.

journeyman
A player who has played for many teams or has been unable to find a specific role.

no-hitter
A complete game in which a pitcher or team doesn't allow any hits.

par
The number of shots a golfer is expected to need to finish a hole.

steroid
A type of drug that athletes are forbidden to use because it can unfairly enhance their performance.

upset
An unexpected victory by a supposedly weaker team or player.

ONLINE RESOURCES

To learn more about the unlikely heroes of sports, visit **abdobooklinks.com**. These links are routinely monitored and updated to provide the most current information available.

MORE INFORMATION

BOOKS

Howell, Brian. *Baseball Trivia*. Minneapolis, MN: Abdo Publishing, 2016.

Myers, Dan. *NFL's Top 10 Plays*. Minneapolis, MN: Abdo Publishing, 2017.

Wilner, Barry. *The Biggest Upsets of All Time*. Minneapolis, MN: Abdo Publishing, 2016.

INDEX

ABOUT THE AUTHOR

Thomas Carothers has been a sportswriter for the past 15 years in the Minneapolis/St. Paul, Minnesota, area. He has worked for a number of print and online publications, mostly focusing on prep sports coverage. He lives in Minneapolis with his wife and a house full of dogs.